First Facts®

Water in Our World

# Saving Water

by Rebecca Olien

raintree

Raintree is an imprint of Capstone Global Library Limited, a company incorporated in England and Wales having its registered office at 264 Banbury Road, Oxford, OX2 7DY – Registered company number: 6695582
**www.raintree.co.uk**
myorders@raintree.co.uk

**Editorial Credits**
Abby Colich, editor; Kyle Grenz, designer; Wanda Winch, media researcher; Laura Manthe, production specialist

**Photo Credits**
Capstone Studio: Karon Dubke, 13; Getty Images, Inc: Justin Sullivan, 9; The Pajaro Valley Water Management Agency: Shinehah Bigham, 14; Shutterstock: Baloncici, 10, Chaoss, 18-19, Cylonphoto, 17, Ecelop, waves design, Migel, 7, Riccardo Mayer, 5, shao weiwei, 20, SKY2015, 1, tachyglossus, splash design, YuryZap, cover

ISBN 978-1-4747-1224-8
19  18  17  16  15
10 9 8 7 6 5 4 3 2 1

**British Library Cataloguing in Publication Data**
A full catalogue record for this book is available from the British Library.

Every effort has been made to contact copyright holders of material reproduced in this book. Any omissions will be rectified in subsequent printings if notice is given to the publisher.

Printed in China.

# Contents

# Sharing water

All living things have to share Earth's water. People, plants and animals need water to live. Only a small amount of Earth's water is safe for people to use. People need to save water by using less.

# Fact!

About 783 million people round the world cannot easily get clean water.

# Freshwater

Many people think there is enough water on Earth. *Salt water* in oceans makes up 97 per cent of Earth's water. But people can't drink salt water.

Only three per cent of Earth's water is *freshwater*. Most freshwater is frozen in *glaciers*. People can only use the freshwater from lakes, rivers and *aquifers*.

salt water—water that is salty; salt water is found in oceans
freshwater—water that has little or no salt; most ponds, rivers, lakes and streams have freshwater
glacier—a large sheet of frozen freshwater; glaciers are found in mountains and polar areas
aquifer—an underground lake

# Laws protect water

Many laws help protect water. Some laws protect freshwater sources. Other laws help keep water clean. Sometimes there are hosepipe bans to *limit* when people can wash their cars and water their gardens.

**limit**—to keep within a certain amount; laws help save water by limiting how much people can use

# Businesses save water

Businesses use millions of litres of water. Factories use water to make items such as paper, cars and other goods. Power stations use water to make electricity.

Many businesses save water by reusing it. Some carwashes save soapy water in underground tanks. The water is cleaned and reused to wash other cars.

# Saving water at home

People can save water at home. To save water, turn off the tap when you brush your teeth. Have shorter showers.

People can save water at home in other ways. Fixing leaky taps and toilets saves water. Using more *efficient* dishwashers and washing machines also saves water.

**efficient**—not wasteful of time or energy

Irrigated with
recycled water

Not for drinking

Pajaro Valley Water
Management Agency

# Saving water outside

Farmers use water to grow crops. To save water, some farmers grow crops that need less water. Other farmers use water that cities *recycle* on their crops.

At home, people use a lot of water outside. To save water, people should only water their gardens when needed. Using your hosepipe less often also saves water.

**recycle**—to use something again

15

# Reusing water

People can reuse water in many ways. Rainwater and waste from sinks and toilets collect in *sewers*. *Water treatment works* clean the water from the sewers. People can then drink the water and use it in their homes.

**sewer**—underground pipes that carry away waste water

**water treatment works**—a place where water is cleaned for people to use at home

a water treatment works

# Saving water

Saving water helps make sure all living things have the freshwater they need. People, plants and animals share the same freshwater. Everyone must work together to save water and keep it clean.

## Fact!

A dripping tap can waste 76 litres (20 gallons) of water a day.

# Amazing but true!

How would you like a cold glass of seawater? Scientists can remove the salt from seawater. Seawater is heated or pushed through a filter to remove the salt. People can drink the water once the salt has been removed.

# Hands on: removing salt

Scientists heat seawater to remove the salt. Try this experiment to see how hot salt water can become freshwater.

## What you need

- 2 teaspoons salt
- clean jar with lid
- hot water

## What you do

1. Place the salt in the jar.
2. Half-fill the jar with hot water from the tap.
3. Put the lid on the jar.
4. Wait 10 minutes.
5. Notice the drops of water forming on the sides and lid of the jar. Carefully remove the lid. Taste the drops on the inside of the lid. Do they taste salty? The water on the lid is evaporated fresh water. The salt stays behind in the jar.

# Glossary

**aquifer**—an underground lake

**efficient**—not wasteful of time or energy

**freshwater**—water that has little or no salt; most ponds, rivers, lakes and streams have freshwater

**glacier**—a large sheet of frozen freshwater; glaciers are found in mountains and polar areas

**limit**—to keep within a certain amount; laws help save water by limiting how much people can use

**recycle**—to use something again

**salt water**—water that is salty; salt water is found in oceans

**sewer**—underground pipes that carry away waste water

**water treatment works**—a place where water is cleaned for people to use at home

# Read more

*Every Last Drop: Bringing Clean Water Home*, Michelle Mulder (Orca Book Publishers, 2014)

*Saving Water* (Environment Detective Investigates), Jen Green (Windmill Books, 2012)

*The Story Behind Water* (True Stories), Christin Ditchfield (Heinemann Library, 2012)

# Websites

**Water facts**
http://www.sciencekids.co.nz/sciencefacts/water.html

**The water family water conservation game**
http://www.thewaterfamily.co.uk/

**The Water Education Foundation water facts for kids**
http://www.watereducation.org/water-kids

# Comprehension questions

1. Why should people try not to waste water?
2. Using online or print resources, list three ways to save water that are not mentioned in the book.
3. Reread page 16 and look at the photo on page 17. Which side is the untreated water from sewers? Which side is the treated water that people can drink?

# Index